Peacocks

by Megan Borgert-Spaniol

BELLWETHER MEDIA • MINNEAPOLIS, MN

Note to Librarians, Teachers, and Parents:

Blastoff! Readers are carefully developed by literacy experts and combine standards-based content with developmentally appropriate text.

Level 1 provides the most support through repetition of high-frequency words, light text, predictable sentence patterns, and strong visual support.

Level 2 offers early readers a bit more challenge through varied simple sentences, increased text load, and less repetition of high-frequency words.

Level 3 advances early-fluent readers toward fluency through increased text and concept load, less reliance on visuals, longer sentences, and more literary language.

Level 4 builds reading stamina by providing more text per page, increased use of punctuation, greater variation in sentence patterns, and increasingly challenging vocabulary.

Level 5 encourages children to move from "learning to read" to "reading to learn" by providing even more text, varied writing styles, and less familiar topics.

Whichever book is right for your reader, Blastoff! Readers are the perfect books to build confidence and encourage a love of reading that will last a lifetime!

This edition first published in 2014 by Bellwether Media, Inc.

No part of this publication may be reproduced in whole or in part without written permission of the publisher. For information regarding permission, write to Bellwether Media, Inc., Attention: Permissions Department, 5357 Penn Avenue South, Minneapolis, MN 55419.

Library of Congress Cataloging-in-Publication Data

Borgert-Spaniol, Megan, 1989-
Peacocks / by Megan Borgert-Spaniol.
  p. cm. – (Blastoff! readers. Animal safari)
  Summary: "Developed by literacy experts for students in kindergarten through grade three, this book introduces peacocks to young readers through leveled text and related photos"– Provided by publisher.
  Audience: K to grade 3.
  Includes bibliographical references and index.
  ISBN 978-1-60014-914-6 (hardcover : alk. paper)
  1. Peafowl–Juvenile literature. I. Title. II. Series: Blastoff! readers. 1, Animal safari.
  QL696.G27B67 2014
  598.6′258–dc23
                                                                    2013000888

Printed in the United States of America, North Mankato, MN.

Contents

What Are Peacocks?

Peacocks are large birds. They live in forests and dry grasslands.

Male peacocks
have bright blue
or green bodies.

Females are called peahens. They are not colorful. This helps them blend in with the ground.

They must hide their **peachicks** from **predators**.

Eating

Peacocks **forage** during the day. They eat plants, **insects**, and fruits.

Roosting

They **roost** in trees. This keeps them safe from predators on the ground.

Tail Feathers

Male peacocks have long tail feathers. These feathers form a **train**.

train

Males fan out their trains for females. The feathers have shiny **eyespots**.

eyespot

19

Females like males with large, bright trains. Looking good, peacock!

21

Glossary

eyespots—colored spots that look like eyes

forage—to go out in search of food

insects—small animals with six legs and hard outer bodies; insect bodies are divided into three parts.

peachicks—baby peacocks

predators—animals that hunt other animals for food

roost—to sleep or rest; peacocks roost in trees to stay safe.

train—the long feathers that trail behind a male peacock as he walks

To Learn More

AT THE LIBRARY

Laminack, Lester L. *Three Hens and a Peacock*. Atlanta, Ga.: Peachtree, 2011.

Marsico, Katie. *A Peachick Grows Up*. New York, N.Y.: Children's Press, 2007.

Underwood, Deborah. *Colorful Peacocks*. Minneapolis, Minn.: Lerner Publications Co., 2007.

ON THE WEB

Learning more about peacocks is as easy as 1, 2, 3.

1. Go to www.factsurfer.com.

2. Enter "peacocks" into the search box.

3. Click the "Surf" button and you will see a list of related Web sites.

With factsurfer.com, finding more information is just a click away.

Index